Praise for Everyone Hates A Ball Hog But They All Love A Scorer

"Coach Godwin's book offers a complete guide to being a team player, both on and off the court."

— *Stack Magazine*

"Coach Godwin's book gives you insight on how to improve your game. If you are a young player trying to get better, this is a book I would recommend reading immediately."

— **Clifford Warren**, *Head Coach Jacksonville University*

"Coach Godwin explains in understandable terms how to improve your game. A must have for any young player hoping to get to the next level."

— **Khalid Salaam**, *Senior Editor, SLAM Magazine*

"I wish that I had this book when I was 16. I would have been a different and better player. Well done."

— **Jeff Haefner**, *Co-owner, BreakthroughBasketball.com*

"The entire book is filled with gems, some new, some revised and some borrowed, but if you want to read one book this year on how to become a better scorer this is the book."

— **Jerome Green**, *Hoopmasters.org*

"Detailed instruction on how to score, preaching that the game is more mental than physical. Good reading for the young set, who might put down that joystick for a few hours."

— *CharlotteObserver.com*

Everyone Hates A Ball Hog But They All Love A Scorer

The Complete Guide To Scoring Points
On and Off the Basketball Court

Coach Koran Godwin

NEW YORK

Everyone Hates A Ball Hog
But They All Love A Scorer

The Complete Guide To Scoring Points On and Off the Basketball Court

by Coach Koran Godwin
© 2010 Koran Godwin. All rights reserved.

ISBN 978-1-60037-712-9 (paperback)
Library of Congress Control Number 2009936502

Published by:

MORGAN · JAMES
THE ENTREPRENEURIAL PUBLISHER ™
www.morganjamespublishing.com

Morgan James Publishing
1225 Franklin Ave. Ste 325
Garden City, NY 11530-1693
Toll Free 800-485-4943
www.MorganJamesPublishing.com

This book is dedicated to my mother, Rhonda who supported me every step of the way. Thanks for planting the seeds of success in my life. I am forever grateful.
You are truly my Hero!!!

Contents

Post-Season

Introduction

I once heard the saying, "Basketball is 80 percent mental and 20 percent physical." Of course, this statement made no sense to me in my early years, because to be honest, most of my scoring came from athleticism and flat-out being better than everyone else my age. I remember putting up 30 points at the age of 12 and thinking to myself, "Man this game is easy." Oh, if only basketball would have stayed that way.

When I entered high school, the game of basketball changed drastically. I was bigger, stronger, and faster, but so was the competition. I remember playing AAU ball for a team named Fast Break in the summer. Coach Chris saw that I was handling the kids my age (15) pretty well, so he decided to move me up to the Under-17 team. This is when I learned that the game of basketball was 80 percent mental.

That summer, I was playing with kids who were taller, faster, and much more athletic. What usually was an uncontested lay-up became a block into the crowd, and the crossover I used against kids my age was ineffective, and many times it was stolen. This was my baptism into the game of basketball. I was paying my dues and I had to find a way to compete.

The next summer, Coach Chris decided to take an interest in me. He coached at perennial basketball powerhouse St. Patrick (New Jersey) and had great knowledge of the game of basketball. He was especially talented at player development and frequently would give lessons to kids in the area who had the money to pay. I never will forget the day in practice when he said, "Be here tomorrow at 4." I said, "Coach, we don't have practice tomorrow." He looked at me and repeated his statement.

I walked into the gym on that hot summer afternoon and was welcomed by two other players who were going to work out. We started off with ball handling, and then went on to jump shooting. Drill after drill, Coach was on us telling us to go harder, faster, stronger. The criticism was intense because there only were three of us. There was nowhere to run or hide my mistakes. Position yourself here; concentrate on your footwork there; I was out of my element but learning at a frantic pace.

What I learned that summer and what you will learn after reading this book is how to score with your mind and not just your feet. Twice a week, he would call the house and say, "I am picking you up in an hour." I would look at my mom and say, "This guy is crazy," but she knew he was giving me the work ethic and direction needed to excel in basketball and life.

By the time I entered my senior year of high school, I was full of knowledge and ready to compete at a high level. I was fortunate that someone saw my potential and was willing to work with me. The lessons learned during those hot summer afternoons stayed with me through college, and they are part of the reason why I started JumpStartHoops.com. Now I get to become your Coach Chris as I share with you what it takes to win and score points on and off the court. Turn the page and get ready to see basketball in a whole new light.

PRE-SEASON

Lesson One

The Godwin Theory

When I look back on all of my accomplishments, one thing stands out: I broke a scoring record at every level I competed. At my high school, I hold the single season scoring record (1998), and at the University of North Florida, I am the all-time leading scorer (2002). Though people always asked the key to my success, I never shared it until now.

Every basketball player wants to be the Big Man on Campus and score a lot of points. Let's face it: from the off the court praise to the media attention and respect, how can you blame them? But my question always is: "Okay, so how do you plan to do it?" What I have found out is that everyone knows what he or she wants to do in life; the problem is finding out how to do it. I, too, faced this dilemma and, being the systematic person that I am, I decided to do something about it.

Like any task or goal that you make for yourself in life, when it is time to plan and mark objectives, you have to break things down into smaller segments. Let's look at a high school basketball game. Most high school games are four eight-minute quarters. Right away, you see that the entire game is 32 minutes long. My approach to every game was simple. I would say to myself if I score four points in eight minutes, then I will end up with 16 points. If I add a free throw in there and score five points a quarter, I will end up with 20 points a game and no doubt become the Big Man on Campus. Right away, my confidence went to the next level as I said to myself, "Who can't score five points in eight minutes?" This simple theory was the breakthrough I was looking for.

When you force yourself to think in quarters, it makes the game look easy. Out of all the ways there are to score the basketball—put back rebound, jump shot, lay-up, free throw—I realized that scoring was more about finding points than having the best jump shot. There is a big difference between a jump shooter and a scorer, and I wanted to join the latter.

This mindset took my game to the next level. In high school, my goal was to score at least six points a quarter. Once I figured out the importance of rebounding, shot selection, and getting to the foul line (subjects that we will go over later in this book), I started to put up huge numbers. The confirmation of my theory occurred when I scored 38 points the second game of my senior year. Three-pointers, lay-ups, foul shots, and offensive rebounds ensured that I gave myself the opportunity to score every time down the floor.

A lot of basketball players shut down when they don't score the way they think they should. How many players do you know rely on one aspect of their game to fill the stat sheet? If their jump shot is not on that day, or people don't get them the ball in the right position, their confidence and game are at a loss. I became a nonpartisan basketball player who would accept any form of scoring that came my way.

In my senior year in high school, I averaged 25 points a game, garnering both a Central Jersey scoring title and a Division 1 scholarship offer to the University of Buffalo. When I got to college, the same rules applied, except instead of four quarters, I now had two halves. My goal every game was to score at least 10 or more before halftime. If I ended the first half with 12 points, I knew I had to score at least eight points in the second half to reach my goal of 20. If I only had four points at halftime, then I knew I had to be more aggressive at the start of the second half.

People always would ask me how I was able to put up big numbers consistently. There were nights in which

I would end up with 25 points scored with only 9 to 12 field goal attempts. The secret was always in my theory. Most basketball players focus on one thing, making all of their shots. If they start off 0 for 4, then their whole game is off because they have the wrong mindset. If I started off a game 0 for 4, then you'd better believe that I would find my way to the free throw line or crash the boards for a cheap put-back rebound.

My shot didn't have any affect on the number of points I scored. What I was looking for was five points a quarter (or 10 points a half). If it was counting pennies at the free throw line, or scoring points in transition I didn't discriminate on how the points came. The newspaper usually said, "Godwin goes for 28." It didn't mention how I did it.

Lesson One: The Godwin Theory

Below is a chart that breaks down The Godwin Theory.

High School: 4 quarters, 8 minutes each quarter

2 Points per Quarter = 8 points per game

3 Points per Quarter = 12 points per game

4 Points per Quarter = 16 points per game

5 Points per Quarter = 20 points per game

6 Points per Quarter = 24 points per game

College: 2 halves, 20 minutes each half

5 Points per Half = 10 points per game

6 Points per Half = 12 points per game

8 Points per Half = 16 points per game

10 Points per Half = 20 points per game

12 Points per Half = 24 points per game

NBA: 4 quarters, 12 minutes each quarter

2 Points per Quarter = 8 points per game

3 Points per Quarter = 12 points per game

4 Points per Quarter = 16 points per game

5 Points per Quarter = 20 points per game

6 Points per Quarter = 24 points per game

 **Coach Godwin Tips**

- Break the game down into quarters and halves.

- Set a reasonable goal to score a certain number of points per quarter.

- Don't rely on one aspect of your game to score points.

- Focus on scoring points and not just getting shots.

- Learn how to score with your mind and not just your feet.

Lesson Two

You Are What You Watch

Most people blame the lack of fundamentals in today's game on ESPN and its 24-hour highlight reel. Older players say that because all kids see are dunks, three-point shots, or crossovers, young players have forgotten (or never knew) how to play the game. Meanwhile, young players argue that basketball has to evolve and they are just doing what they know. I can relate to the mentalities of both the young and old.

The truth of the matter is that both sides are right, because you are what you watch. There comes a time in every basketball player's career that he or she realizes the importance of studying film. As a young player coming up, I chose to study Michael Jordan. I would study everything from his shooting form to his offensive moves, and even his off-season workout plan. I bought his DVDs and to this day I can look in my video collection and find all types of film from his glory days. When every other kid was in the park practicing his famed highlight, the reverse lay-up, I was focused on how he got past the defender to get in position to perform his patented move.

Learning how to emulate what you see is a very important aspect of scoring. This is why people always say you should play against players who are older and better than you. They tell you this because experienced players and coaches know that the more you play, the more you will pick up. Playing against experienced people gives you the opportunity to observe and duplicate what makes them successful. The same is true when it comes to watching game film.

I never will forget the day my Jordan studying days paid off. I was a freshman at the University of Buffalo and it was time to get ready for Miami of Ohio. Just like clockwork, the first thing we do to prepare for a team is watch their game film. The session starts off with watching the opposing team's plays; then we focus on position-specific film. Being that I was a guard, our sole focus was to stop an All-American player from Long Island named Wally Szczerbiak.

Standing 6-foot-7 and weighing 240 pounds, Wally was a tough match up for any guard. He was tearing up the competition and we heard before the game that NBA scouts from Toronto were coming to evaluate him. As a 6-foot-3 freshman, I saw the opportunity to compete against Szczerbiak as a way to find the secret to his success. I studied his game film intently, taking mental notes of everything he did.

The first thing I noticed was that Szczerbiak was not a world-class athlete. Yes, he had the size and jump shot, but he was far from the Michael Jordan/Kobe Bryant type I was used to studying or playing against in New

Jersey. What captured my attention was that Szczerbiak truly scored with his head and not his feet. This was the enlightening because all my life I was led to believe that you have to be at least a B athlete to become a great scorer. This couldn't have been farther from the truth.

Clip after clip, Szczerbiak was destroying the competition. Since everyone scouts and has his game film, I soon noticed that his game was more that just his pure jump shot. He mastered the triple threat in a way that I had not seen before. Whether the defender pressed him or played off, it seemed that Szczerbiak had a natural progression in his mind. He never looked rushed and always took what the defense gave him. My new goal was to be able to do the same.

What I learned from Szczerbiak is the value of slowing down the game and picking your spots. As I continued to watch the film, I noticed that most of his shots came from calculated half-court moves and great footwork. He would get in his triple-threat position, lull you to sleep, and explode to the basket to finish a lay-up or knock down his automatic pull-up jump shot.

I fell in love with his game because we had a similar skill set. I, too, had a jump shot that ranged well beyond the three-point arc and a knack for scoring with my head. Since he was where I wanted to be, I had no problem following every one of his games, looking for ways to get better. No matter who you choose to emulate remember, you are what you watch.

# Coach Godwin Tips

◈ **Find someone who is successful and study his or her game film.**

◈ **Pay attention to the subtle details that make that person successful.**

◈ **If you see something you like, implement it in your game.**

Lesson Three

Graduating from Shooter to Scorer

My Szczerbiak epiphany couldn't have come at a better time in my career. The spring of my senior year in high school, I made a terrible mistake. While going to play pickup ball at the Dunn Center in Elizabeth, New Jersey, I forgot to wear my ankle braces and ended up paying for it with a severely sprained ankle. The doctor said I had chipped a bone in my ankle and stretched ligaments. He said that it would heal eventually, but not as fast due to my still being active. This completely changed my life because now I had the dubious task of playing Division 1 college basketball without the athleticism that helped me put up 25 points a game in high school.

But Szczerbiak had shown me that I didn't need athleticism to score. The most potent scorers are those who score with their minds. I likened it to the basketball difference between an shooter and a scorer. A shooter is someone who goes out and just uses his/her jump shot to score. There is no plan or direction; he or she gets the ball and shoots it. A scorer is someone who takes his/her time, identifies the weakness in the defense, and attacks accordingly. It's like playing the game of chess. Every move is calculated and has its purpose.

With limited athleticism, I was forced to get back to the fundamentals that Coach Chris taught me during those summer workouts in St. Patrick's gym. Coming off of screens and picking my spots became my trademark. Since I was a dead eye shooter, the only thing stopping me from scoring was getting open.

Every practice was another opportunity to figure out how I was going to get my points. Without great athleticism, it was next to impossible to get those rebounds that I made a living off of in high school. I recall playing against North Carolina and trying to get a rebound over 7¬foot-2 Brendon Haywood. I soon realized I needed to find a new way to score.

What I learned was that there were certain spots and situations on the floor that were impossible to guard. In transition, you are taught to stop the ball and protect the basket from easy lay-ups; this was the opportunity I was waiting for. In transition, when my point guard got the ball, I would sprint to the corner. I found that this is the one spot on the floor that no one defends on a fast break. In fact, every position beyond the three-point line sets you up for a wide-open shot because the defense has to recover to the paint.

At the University of Buffalo, I was instant offense off of the bench. Everything came together one winter night. We were playing Central Michigan, one of our conference foes and I was excited for the match up. The only problem was that I still had a bad ankle and my lateral movement was limited. I tried as hard as I could to hide myself on defense, but the coaches saw right through it; consequently, my playing time was sparse.

Central Michigan got out to an early lead on us, and my coach was looking for answers. He looked down the bench and said, reluctantly, "Godwin, get in there." I was never nervous, mainly because I figured, "Hey, if I make any mistakes, it will go into the, aw, he-is-an¬inexperienced-freshman pile." As soon as I hit the floor, I had one thing on my mind: finding the open spot. It was our ball and we were taking it out under our basket. The play was designed for me to set a screen, but I chose otherwise.

With my assistant coach yelling at the top of his lungs to run the play, I drifted out to the three-point line and waved my hands in the air. My point guard passed me the ball and right away I shot it. It hit nothing but the bottom of the net. I came down again and, since we had a motion offense, I had free rein to utilize a screen. Swoosh, another 3. In five minutes, I ended up with 12 points on my way to a 26-point game. My metamorphosis was validated, I learned how to become a scorer on the college level.

 **Coach Godwin Tips**

◆ Find out if you are a shooter or scorer.

◆ Make a goal to study the game and become a scorer.

◆ Find multiple ways to score points.

◆ Ask the question: How can I score more points? The answers will come.

Lesson Four

The Locker Room View

The game of basketball is played at many speeds. Each game is affected by a variety of factors, including coaching philosophy, referee calls, and player personnel. As a player, I would try to figure out the pace of the game before I played in it. In high school, most teams are known for playing a certain way, and in college, you get to study your opponents' game film before you compete. These all give advantages to the scorer because you want to have a visual of where your points are going to come from each game.

If you know you are playing a fast-paced team that likes to run up and down the floor, then most of your points are going to come in transition. If the team is known for slowing down the game, then you know that a lot of your opportunities are going to come from half-court sets. Do your homework so you can pass the test.

Having these forecasts in place allows you to visualize what is going to happen when you hit the court. This is one of the less talked about aspects of becoming a great scorer. My mother used to say that in order to be it, you have to see it. Before any game, you have to visualize yourself in different scoring positions. Lay-ups, 15-foot jump shots, dribble drive to the basket: play them all in your head over and over again.

Visualization is power. It allows your mind and body to get ready for what you are going to do on the court. I can remember going on trips for away games and watching my teammates crack jokes and cut up in the locker room. I always would say to myself: how do you expect to perform at a high level if you are not visualizing the task at hand? The problem is that a lot of players don't understand the concept of visualization; they just go out and see what happens. That may work for some, but I tell you now: if you don't have a plan in place, you are setting yourself up for inconsistent results.

When you are in the locker room, you want to get into your zone. Whatever you have to do to focus on the game is up to you. I used to listen to my Walkman to help me separate myself from what was going on around me. Most of my teammates knew not to talk to me around game time because I wouldn't talk back. I was in a zone and unless the building was on fire, I didn't want to hear anything.

If there was any example of how you should conduct yourself before a game, it would be observing Kevin Garnett. I love the fact that even though he makes millions of dollars, he still takes the time to separate himself from the surroundings and visualize before the game. A few minutes before the game, Garnett goes into a zone that is second to none. With that kind of mindset, he is poised to perform every night, and the fans always get their money's worth.

 **Coach Godwin Tips**

❖ **Separate from your surroundings so you can visualize. Tune everyone out.**

❖ **Always visualize positive results: dunks, lay-ups, steals, three-point shots.**

❖ **Try to see where your points are going to come from: the paint, transition, half-court sets, etc...**

❖ **Do your homework about the team you are playing so you know what to visualize.**

GAME TIME

Lesson Five

Coach Godwin's
Speed Theory

This probably is the most important part of the book. In my DVD *Fundamentals of Scoring*, I go over the theory that allowed me to score points night in and night out. Let's take a deeper look into the details of my speed theory.

In basketball, being quick is the ability to start, stop, and start again. This is completely different from being fast, which is your ability to run at a steady pace. To measure quickness, look at your body like a gearshift in a car: 1. Walking/Standing; 2. Jogging; 3. Running; 4. Accelerating at top speed. Everyone possesses all four speeds, but my theory teaches you how to use them. Most basketball players think they have to use their four speed all of the time to get things done. This couldn't be farther from the truth. Just as in a car, the faster you are going, the less control you have over your body. If you go into four speed every time you get the ball, you soon will find that success will come only from making brash decisions.

Lesson Five: Coach Godwin's Speed Theory

To become a great scorer, you want to be able to see the game in slow motion. Check out all of the greats from Michael Jordan to Kobe Bryant and you will find they never were in a rush and used their control of speed to dominate the game. The key is only using your four speed for a purpose. You only go there when you want to get something accomplished. The rest of the time you should put you gearshift into third. This will allow you to penetrate the defense and get out of trouble when needed.

When you watch most college games, you will see players zooming up and down the court in four speed, thinking that is the way to score points. Flip the channel to an NBA game and you will find that the only time the four speed is utilized is when it's time to get to the basket. That is why it is easy for me to spot an NBA-ready player on the college level. The announcer usually uses the phrase "calm and collective," but what he really is seeing is a kid who knows how and when to use his four speed. I remember watching short clips of Carmelo Anthony and Brandon Roy and saying to myself: both of these guys will be successful in the NBA because they understand speed control.

When you have control of your speed, you are almost impossible to stop. This is because only you know where and when you are going to accelerate to the basket. Defenders love it when you start off using your four speed because they now can gauge your speed and stay with you, but when you come down the court in three speed and make a quick crossover to four, it takes a very disciplined and athletic guy to stay in front of you.

I remember when I transferred to the University of North Florida (to get out of 62 inches of snow) and began noticing the difference in competition. Where the Midwest-based Mid American Conference (MAC) focused on basketball IQ, the South was full of tremendous athletes. The speed theory was more important than ever because, though I was getting some of my athleticism back from my ankle injury, my four speed was average, at best.

The thing I noticed most is that, though many were more athletic with one fake in the opposite direction, my control of four speed forced guys to overreact. In my second or third game as a sophomore, I scored 32 points against a cross-town rival, and it was all due to picking my spots and controlling my body speed.

A lot of the success from the speed theory comes out of the triple-threat position. This is because you are in a position to go from standing still to four speed in the blink of an eye. The key is your ability to lull your defender to sleep and utilize your jab step to get him or her off balance. No matter how quick the defender is, if you get him to lean one way or relax with his heels on the floor, he is at a disadvantage.

One of my tactics for the triple-threat position was always to act like I was trying to pass the ball to someone. What I really was doing was looking for driving angles and lulling my defender to sleep. When the defender thinks you are trying to pass the ball, he is less likely to concentrate on stopping an explosive move. It works every time!

Lesson Five: Coach Godwin's Speed Theory

I recall playing against a guy who was hell-bent on stopping me from scoring. I could tell because every time I touched the ball, his teammates on the bench would get up to hype him up to guard me. This was rather amusing to me because he was expending a lot of energy trying to make it difficult for me to score. Pass after the pass, I would catch the ball and never look like I wanted to score. Consequently, he became overconfident and I exploded past him from one to four speed for a pull-up jump shot. I looked at his bench and they all sat down. Then I looked at the defender and he looked down, knowing it was going to be a long day.

 # Coach Godwin Tips

- Learn how to utilize your one through four speeds.

- Only use speed four for a purpose.

- In triple threat, lull your defender to sleep and explode from one to four.

- See the driving angles before you use your four speed. Avoid being out of control.

- See your body as a gearshift!!!

Lesson Six

Convincing Your Teammates

One of the hardest things to do in life is handling success. Whether it involves getting your first double-double or having your first 30-point performance, going from nothing to something can be challenging. Some people will like you for scoring all the points and some people will hate you for scoring all the points. There are two names that you will hear after you start to excel consistently at a high level: ball hog or scorer. Though they are one and the same, their perceptions can make or break your career.

The ball hog is a guy who over dribbles, never passes the ball, and always seems to want to shoot every time he touches the ball. There is no problem with wanting to score; hey, if you don't score you don't win, but there is a way you have to do it. You see, everyone hates a ball hog. The ball goes to this guy and one thing is certain: it is not coming back out.

The major issue that I have with the ball hog tag is that no one wants to play with you. Yeah, a lot of guys feel that they don't need their teammates, but I beg to differ. If you can *convince* your teammates and coach that you are a scorer, then this will make your life a whole lot easier.

A scorer is someone who has a knack for being around the ball and putting it in the basket. Whether it's a post player down low who scores with post moves and put-backs or a guard who scores with outside shots, a scorer gets the job done. Notice, I used the word *convince* when I talked about the difference between a ball hog and scorer. The bottom line is they both put up a ton of shots, but they have a different perception.

If you want to shake the ball hog stigma, you have to master your shot selection. The reason many players are called ball hogs is because they take terrible shots. Even if it goes in, the average observer is going to look at your success as a selfish act. This is where studying the game comes into play.

As a player, the first thing I would do is study the coach's system. Unlike pickup ball, every coach has an idealistic way of running a team. He has plays that he swears will work in any situation, and it's up to you to find a way to score with them. What I found is that no matter what system I play in, if you know how to get open, no one can complain even though you end up taking a majority of the shots.

I recall running the flex, which is a universal basketball offense of screens and cuts. Since I was more skilled at using screens and back cuts then some of my teammates, I always would end up taking the shot. When I was having an off day, my coach would say,

"Godwin, pass the ball," and my reply always would be an irrefutable, "but I was open."

As a coach, this sometimes comes back to haunt me when I yell at a kid who just missed his last two shots and he turns around and says he was wide open. I can't help but chuckle because I know that unless you tell a kid not to shoot the ball, he is right. If you want to evade the ball hog scarlet letter, there are some golden rules to follow.

 **Coach Godwin Tips**

- **Never look like you want to score:**
  Every time you get the ball, keep your
  head up and fake like you want to pass
  the ball even if your intentions are to
  shoot the ball.

- **Be willing to pass the ball, especially
  in practice:** Take practice as the time to
  develop team chemistry and trust from
  your teammates. The coach wants to run
  every play through, so use this as an
  opportunity to shed the ball hog tag.

- **Learn how to come off of screens:**
  Learning how to come off of screens made
  me a constant threat. Every coach expects

you to shoot when your man is caught up in the screen.

- Learn how to set screens: The quickest way to get open is setting a screen. When two people are confused about whom they are guarding, someone always is wide open.

- Be Quick but Not in a Rush: Nothing looks better then a guy who is under control.

Lesson Seven

Finding Points

If you want to become a prolific scorer, you have to learn how to find loose points. The most inconsistent scorers are those who rely on a few aspects of the game to score. I can't tell you how much it frustrates me to see a gifted basketball player rely solely on his jump shot to score. The problem with the jump shot is that no matter how good a shooter you think you are, there always will be days when your shot just isn't falling. There also will be days when your defender will limit quality shot opportunities. There are three ways to score that never will fail you. They are offensive rebounding, easy lay-ups, and the free throw line.

Offensive Rebounding

Offensive rebounding is a sure fire way to score. The defense always is out of position to guard you because their attention is on the basket and their back is to you. This is a great opportunity to shoot an uncontested shot. When I found this out in high school, my scoring average went through the roof. I averaged more than 11 rebounds a game, and most of them came from the offensive boards.

As a scorer, you always are in position to box out your defender because he is concentrating on you, not the ball. I remember playing a game in which the opposing coach played a box-and-one on me. The box-and-one is a defense designed to stop one player from even touching the ball. It is effective against teams that rely on one player to score a lot of points, as was the case with my team. So what I did was move around as if I wanted the ball, and when a teammate shot it, I would box out my man who was denying me and rebound the ball for a put-back or plus-one. That game, I ended up with over 24 points and the coach was left scratching his head.

Easy Lay-ups

Easy lay-ups also are a great way to pad your stats. Whether in transition or the half court, lay-ups usually come from being in the right place at the right time. Both of my college point guards were assist junkies, so I found myself with plenty of chip shots to add to the average.

Back door cuts, offensive rebounds, broken plays: I see them all as opportunities to put the ball in the basket. Remember, a scorer has a knack for being around the ball.

Free Throw Line

The psychology of scoring is no different than life. The better your start, the greater chance you have of success later on. Most of your success comes from your confidence, which as we all know fluctuates from play to play. As a way to gain confidence, I would try to get to the line as early as possible. As a scorer, I feed off seeing the ball go through the net. I can be having a horrible shooting night, but give me one free throw and I think I am on fire again.

In the first quarter of each game, I want to draw as many fouls as possible. For one thing, it helps your team by getting the opposing starters in foul trouble. It also gives you the opportunity to break the ice by scoring at the foul line. Now my confidence is high and I am ready to shoot the ball more often.

Another advantage is that your defender now has a foul. Every player knows that the golden rule is: two fouls in the first half and you have to sit. No coach wants to risk not having his or her key player for the second half. This means that my defender now has to give me what I want. Whether it is an uncontested jump shot or another easy drive to the basket, I am in position to get what I want. It also helps you score against the next person to guard you because he saw what happened to his teammate.

It is very important that you work hard at becoming a great free throw shooter. I used to spend hours at the end after practice shooting hundreds of free throws because I knew they were good for 8 to 12 points every night. I was so good at free throws that the local newspaper actually had an article highlighting my over 90 percent free throw percentage. The free throw line saved me when my shot was not going in or was hard to get off.

This is the one place that you control your own destiny without someone trying to stop you. Getting to the free throw line is an art. It involves some acting, success, and a whole lot of moxie. Whenever I was able to get a defender in the air with my pump fake, I would lean into his body and make him foul me. Once you master the ball fake, you are a couple of acting lessons away from getting to the line game after game.

 **Coach Godwin Tips**

◈ **Look for loose points.**

◈ **Always attack the offensive boards.**

◈ **Learn how to hover around the basket for lay-up opportunities.**

◈ **Work on your free throws and getting to the line.**

◈ **Use your ball fake to draw fouls.**

◈ **Work on those acting skills.**

Lesson Eight

Knowing When to Pass the Ball

Passing the ball probably is the hardest thing to do when you are known to be a big time scorer, but it has many advantages. The first advantage is keeping your teammates happy. There is no harder feat then trying to go out night after night and do it all yourself. It takes a toll on your body and mind because you are taking on more than you can handle. Doing it all yourself is a short-term solution to a long-term problem.

Because I started scoring a lot of points at a young age, I was able to see the effects of thinking I could do everything myself. I remember being on a team with a point guard who gave me the ball every time down the floor. I averaged more than 30 points a game and we were winning the majority of the time. The only problem was that my teammates were less inclined to play defense and never gained any confidence offensively because I was shooting the ball every play.

I was having fun until I realized it was taking a toll on my body. Scoring 30 points a game is very hard when you're getting double-teamed and fouled all game. There are no easy baskets and it gets tougher when you take a beating game after game.

Going into the playoffs, we were favorites to win the championship, until the recreation league implemented a new rule saying I could play only two quarters. Now, my teammates, who rarely shot the ball, had to fend for themselves as I only could look from the sidelines. To make a long story short, we lost in the playoffs because I was trying to do it all myself. This is when I learned that I had to find a way to keep my teammates happy, even though I was going to shoot the ball the majority of the time.

Another advantage to passing the ball is that it opens opportunities for you to score. Whenever a coach sees an opponent who is reluctant to pass, all he has to do is double-team him. The hardest guy to guard is a scorer who can find the open man. It keeps everyone else honest and limits the strategy of the opposing coach. This is why it is so important to study the game and come up with more than one way to score. If you want to become the ultimate threat, learn how to score with and without the ball in your hands, and always be willing to pass the ball to the open man.

 **Coach Godwin Tips**

- Don't try to do it all yourself.

- Pass the ball to open teammates to avoid the double-team strategy.

- Keep your teammates happy by including them in the offense.

- Try not to be the one pass and shot player who ruins team chemistry.

Lesson Nine

Now That They Know Who You Are

Once you get a name for yourself, you would think that scoring gets harder. Coaches prepare their players night and day with the keys to stopping you from putting up big numbers. They have game film, advice from other coaches, and stats from your previous games. It seems that they have your number, but I am going to show you how to use these factors to score even more points.

I used to love these tactics of preparation to stop me because they introduced the one thing that made it easier for me to score points: FEAR. There is nothing worse than knowing you have the task of stopping the leading scorer on the opposing team. Every coach makes it seem that if you just do these four simple things, you will stop this guy from scoring, and your teammates constantly tease you because they know you have to stop someone who is known for being unstoppable. On the bus before and after the game, there always is a review of what happened during the game, with your teammates highlighting the embarrassing moments. This is a position no player is comfortable being in.

Lesson Nine: Now That They Know Who You Are

I got a kick out of being captain because nine times out of ten, the opposing captain had the duty of guarding me on defense. I always could spot my defender because he never wanted to look me in the eye. He already knew everything about me and had stayed up half the night trying to figure out a way to execute and do what his coach said would work.

The truth of the matter is you can't stop an scorer with a high basketball IQ. You could be the best defender on the planet and know all of my favorite moves. What you don't realize is that I am going to adjust to you and take what you give me, not what you saw on tape. Do you know how frustrating it is to play solid defense, hold a scorer to only two field goals made in the first half, and still have him finish with 12 points? It will drive you crazy!

The combination of fear and anticipation is too much for anyone to handle. With each shot that goes in, I am taking a chunk of confidence from my defender. Better than that, when he has to go to the bench because of his ineffectiveness or foul trouble, the confidence of the next guy behind him already is low because he saw what I did to their best defender. What the coach really should say is: "Look, we are not going to stop this guy from scoring, but we are going to make him work for everything he gets." This philosophy pays better dividends because a lot of scorers will suffer defensively due to all the energy being spent on offense.

Lesson Nine: Now That They Know Who You Are

Another advantage is that in basketball, sometimes the rich get richer. The other team's players aren't the only ones who know your name; the referees know who you are, too. Every referee appreciates someone who knows how to play the game, and don't think for a second that doesn't make them more inclined to blow their whistles when you drive to the basket. I remember getting at least five questionable calls a game. Of course, I helped by always overreacting to every bit of contact, but, hey, a foul is a foul; the referee can't take it back.

The way I saw it, those five calls equated to at least eight points a game. When you are a bona fide scorer, you always get the benefit of the doubt. Watch any NBA game and you will notice that you see the top players on the foul line the most. When a rookie drives and gets fouled, there's no call, but as soon as Joe All-Star drives, the whistle is blown before you touch him. I guess success begets success.

 **Coach Godwin Tips**

- Use the opposing coach's strategy to instill fear in your defenders.

- Think like an scorer.

- Drive to the hole to draw fouls.

- Use your name and success to get to the foul line.

POST-SEASON

Lesson Ten

The Off-Season

I once heard a quote from Henry Clay that changed my work ethic on and off the court: "The time will come when winter will ask you what you were doing all summer." This statement hit home as I noticed that the difference between a good player and a great player was how hard he worked. This is the reason I prided myself on work ethic and dedication in the off-season.

Since I was fortunate enough to have someone teach me the game, all I had to do was my part. Each day I wasn't working out with Coach Chris I would go to the park and practice the drills he was teaching me. Since I didn't have a gym to go to, I would take my basketball and dribble all around the neighborhood on my way to the court. Between the legs, crossovers, spin moves: I would make sure that I developed a relationship with the basketball. When I got to the court, I would practice my shooting form and free throws. After that I would implement everything I learned from Coach and create my own workout.

A lot of kids my age used think I was overdoing it, but they didn't see what I saw. The off-season was my advantage, my time to get better and come back a more polished player. I honestly can say that there was no three¬day period of time when I didn't have the basketball in my hands. It became my passion and my hobby.

The most important reason you should develop a work ethic is confidence. There is a certain swagger that comes with knowing that no one on the floor did what you did in the off-season. I recall being asked why I shoot the ball so much, and my reply was because in the summer I am shooting 1,000 shots a day. The way I saw it, I deserve to shoot the ball more than anyone else.

In college, before every game, I would be the first one dressed in my uniform so I could go to the auxiliary gym and put up at least 100 shots before the game. By the time I shot the ball during the game, I already was on my 200th shot. Many people just look at my stats, but if they only knew what it took to get them.

To become effective, you must be able to identify the weaknesses in your game and work on them tirelessly in the off-season. In high school, I was a pure shooter and could put the ball in the hole with ease, but my ball handling skills were lacking. This proved to be a major problem because the top point guard was a year ahead of me, which left the ball handling duties up in the air my senior year.

That summer, I worked on my dribbling like a madman because I foresaw what was going to happen. If my ball handling didn't improve, my team and stats were going to suffer. During my senior year, although I was a two guard, I was able to bring the ball up the floor when called upon. This helped out tremendously because I added a new facet that made me a Division 1 basketball player.

Lesson Ten: The Off-Season

Another important part of the off-season is working in the weight room. There used to be an old myth that lifting weights would throw off your jump shot. That is, until the greatest player to play the game, Michael Jordan, admitted that he lifts weights year-round, sometimes even on game days.

Getting quicker, faster, stronger, and more durable is top priority. Lifting weights helps with injury prevention, strength, and mental toughness. Half of the things that you are reading in this book will not help you if you are not strong enough to put yourself in position to score.

Today, you have to be in that weight room if you want to compete. There are guys nowadays who make you wonder if they are better suited to play football than basketball. On the college level if you are not strong, you will get eaten alive. I remember my first college practice when the ball was taken right out of my hands. Being that I was a freshman, I didn't know that coaches neglected to call fouls as a means to get you tougher for the game. My weight training in the off-season paid off, as I had to adjust to playing without the foul being called.

I look back on my high school game film from sophomore to senior year and I can't help but laugh. What it told me was that I was serious about my body and getting stronger. After putting on a couple of pounds, I was ready to take the pounding necessary to put points on the board every night. Since a lot of my points came from offensive rebounding and the free throw line, I had to have the strength to overpower those who didn't heed the off-season work ethic.

The first thing I noticed after a couple of months in the weight room was a boom in my confidence. Though I was 6-foot-3 and a bit over 180 pounds, in my head I was Shaq. There is not a position on the floor in high school that I didn't think I could play, and that was due to the weights. I was confident and relentless on the boards. I averaged a double double, which is rare for a shooting guard with a pure jump shot. The weight room made me aggressive every night.

After I sustained an ankle injury that almost ended my career, I used the same off-season work ethic to recover. The University of North Florida had an excellent staff that taught me how to strengthen my ankles to get some of my athleticism back. I took those therapy sessions and implemented them at home in my summer workout. My sophomore year in college I averaged close to 18 points a game, but I knew that I was playing on 60 percent of what I had in high school. It was a horrible feeling playing above the rim and suddenly having to rely on basketball IQ alone, so I did something about it.

That summer, along with my personal therapy sessions, I implemented a leg workout that was second to none. I worked overtime on the squat machine and it paid big dividends. By the time we had our physical test, my two-foot vertical was at a staggering 36 inches. Now, I was able reach the 11-foot mark and my dunking days were back. My athleticism was back and my off-season work paid off with a scoring title my junior year.

Coach Godwin Tips

- Find your weaknesses and work on them tirelessly.

- Make it a goal to come back a more polished player.

- Hit the weight room and hit it hard!

- Use the weight room to boost your confidence and aggression.

- Incorporate those squats for a total body workout and increase your vertical.

Lesson Eleven

The Fundamentals

It amazes me how many basketball players want to run before they can walk. Because of the success of a few stellar athletes, a lot of kids grow up thinking that they can bypass the fundamentals of the game. We now live in an era in basketball where if you have size or can jump out of the gym, people attach the "potential" tag to your name and crown you the NBA's next star.

The sad part about this scenario is that many kids now feel that working on their ball handling, footwork, and jump shot is taboo. If it doesn't come natural, then they don't need it. They believe that the players who can dunk from the free throw line are the ones who get to sign big contracts and shoe deals. Please do not fall into this category.

I am here to tell you that what you see on television is the exception, not the rule. Mastering the fundamentals always will put you in a better position to get a scholarship or, if you're blessed enough, grace an NBA floor. The last thing you want to do is limit yourself to only what God has given you. There are plenty of camps, books, and instructional videos; take advantage of them.

Lesson Eleven: The Fundamentals

The most glaring oversight has been the lack of shooting technique. You would think that in a game that relies solely on your ability to put the ball in the basket, players would focus on their shooting form. Yes, there are cases in which a player may have taught him/herself how to shoot, but with the advent of the Internet and video instruction, there are no excuses. If you want to learn in today's world, all you need is Google.

In my DVD, *The Fundamentals of Shooting*, I go through all the steps to become a great shooter. I break down the technique through a progression I call the 3 Fs: footwork, form, and follow through. The key to becoming a great shooter after you understand the proper form is the timing of your release. Most people say: shoot at the top of your jump shot, but what does that mean? Jump my highest and shoot? No. As your feet are leaving the floor, you are using that momentum to push the ball out of your hands. In essence, you are shooting the ball with your legs and the proper form.

A lot of players these days have trouble with their footwork, form, and follow through. I suggest that if this is you, find out the right way to shoot. Knowledge is power. Once you know, then you are a great work ethic away from lighting up the scoreboard. The worst thing you can do is combine work ethic with a lack of direction. You will find yourself creating a plethora of bad habits that will be harder to correct in the future.

Coach Godwin Tips

- **Focus on the fundamentals of Ball Handling, Jump Shooting, Post Play, etc...**

- **Many NBA stars are the exception, not the rule. Don't believe the hype.**

- **Seek a shooting coach or video.**

- **Absorb instruction from coaches or teammates who excel in areas you are weak in.**

Lesson Twelve

Focus on Go-to Moves

After you understand the importance of a strong work ethic, it's time to master the moves that the pros use to score in bunches. With experience, you learn to simplify and break down everything you do in life. Basketball is no different. There are a couple of moves that, when performed correctly, are next to impossible to guard, so lets take a look at a few of them.

The Step Back (*The Fundamentals of Scoring DVD*).

Far and away, this is my favorite half-court move. I love this move because it is one of the few ways to get your shot off when and where you want. It is the ultimate space creator and is effective against both quick and long defenders.

Whenever I had a strong quick defender who prided himself on cutting off penetration, I would accelerate to my four speed on an angle, push off low as soon as the defender went to cut me off, and step back into my jump shot. This move is very frustrating for the defender because it works even if he is playing perfect textbook defense. I can't tell you how many times this move has gotten me out of trouble.

Swinging Through (detailed in *The Fundamentals of Scoring*).

This move is effective because it starts with your back to the defender. Whether you are coming off a screen or in the mid-post, if you execute this move correctly, it is almost impossible to stop. With your defender behind you, catch the ball on the wing, immediately establish your pivot, and swing the ball through attacking the baseline. The defender always is at a disadvantage because his momentum is pushing him toward you while you are pivoting and driving past him.

Jump Hook (*The Fundamentals of Post Play DVD*).

The jump hook is used primarily in the post area. I love this move because it ensures that you always will get your shot off. After a drop step, usually toward the middle off the paint, you turn your shoulders parallel to the sideline and shoot the ball over your defender. If you perform this move properly, your body will be in between the ball and your defender. When you master shooting your hook off of body contact, this move gives you a chance to get fouled and go to the line.

 **Coach Godwin Tips**

- Focus on the moves that are hard to defend.

- Always have at least two moves that you know will allow you to get your shot off.

- Master the **STEP BACK, JUMP HOOK** and **SWING THROUGH.**

Lesson Thirteen

Seeking Knowledge

The great scorers understand the importance of increasing their basketball IQ. Whether it is from reading books or watching basketball instructional videos, your quest for knowledge should never end. In basketball, the more you know, the easier it will be to score points and help your team win on and off the court.

If you look at any NBA roster every now and then, you will find a player who is twice the age of the rookies coming in but still seems to have decent statistics. I can remember a guy asking why in the world would they keep these old players around when there is fresh young talent overseas and in college waiting to get their opportunity to play in the league. The answer is simple: the 15-year veterans come with extremely high basketball IQs and the wisdom of knowing how to get the job done more efficiently.

Having a high basketball IQ is many times more important than what you can do athletically. Players who are smart make fewer mistakes, and they understand how to score in any situation. If the coach says run the play through; the scorer is intelligent enough to set quality screens knowing he eventually will get open for an easy lay-up. The coach says do not shoot the ball unless we get an opportunity for a lay-up, and he sets his man up to go back door. Every fan, teammate, and coach loves a smart basketball player.

When I accepted the offer to transfer to the University of North Florida, the first thing I asked the coach was, " Who is the point guard?" Coach told me that he averaged more than 10 assists a game in high school and probably would start as a freshman. If he could only have seen the smile on my face…

My first objective when I got on campus was to embrace this incoming freshman who had a knack for dishing out assists. I knew that the key to my success was developing a relationship with the guy who was going to be passing me the ball for the next three years. I said to myself that he was going to be the Robin to my Batman, and, boy, was I right.

Midway through my sophomore year I was averaging close to 20 points a game. Although my freshman point guard lacked athleticism, he had a very high basketball IQ. We were on the same page and he made sure he knew where I was at all times. If he penetrated, I flared out for an easy three-point shot. If the defender was overplaying me, I gave him eye contact, then went back door for an easy lay-up. If I was having trouble getting an open look, he would call a play so I could set my man up for a curl off the screen. I ended up using half of the energy I normally did in high school, and the results were consistent every night.

Lesson Thirteen: Seeking Knowledge

It was a pleasure playing with someone who knew the game as well as I did. We both wanted to get better and talked basketball daily. From analyzing players in the NBA to the ones we were going to play against, our thirst for knowledge made us successful on the court. It is no coincidence that he became the all-time leader in assists. Hey, I was more than happy to help him out with that accomplishment!

 **Coach Godwin Tips**

- **Always seek knowledge.**

- **Watch a lot of basketball.**

- **Talk to those who share your desire to learn more. Develop a strong relationship with your teammates, especially your point guard.**

Lesson Fourteen

Scoring Off the Court

Mental preparation and basketball/life balance are essential to scoring points consistently year after year. Every basketball player must prioritize his/her life so that when things happen off the court, they don't affect you on the court. It is up to you to find your balance and priorities.

As I was coming up as a pre-teen in New Jersey, I witnessed many talented players waste their God-given ability on lack or focus and balance. What I found out was that their off-the-court issues translated to negative and inconsistent results on the floor. That was when I decided that if I was going to get a scholarship and play at a high level, I had better set some rules and parameters.

My priorities were simple: God, family, school, and then basketball. My faith in God as a Christian gave me purpose and made me realize that everything I accomplished is to the glory of God. When you really look at it, no one has control over what talents God gives him or her. We all just play the hand we are dealt and try to win at the game of life.

I always remembered that the Lord can give you something and he also can take it away. Case in point: my eventual career-ending ankle injury that I sustained soon after my senior season was over. Here I am on top of the world. I lead the area in scoring, made the North/South New Jersey All-Star game, and was receiving a lot of attention from Division 1 coaches. With one twist of the ankle, I found myself on the floor almost in tears hoping I didn't just ruin my chances of playing at the school of my choice.

What God was saying to me was that I am to keep him first. Many players lose their character because of the hype and attention you get when you are a basketball star. They don't understand that you have to take everything with a grain of salt because it all could be over any minute. At the tender age of 12, I made Jesus Christ my Lord and Savior, and never looked back. He is the true gift to the world.

My family was second on the list. My mother taught me at a young age to never give up and always finish what I had started. When I was 8, my mother asked me if I wanted to play football. Being the average 8-year⌐old who knows absolutely nothing about what he wants to do in life, I took the easy route and said no. The next week my mother dropped me off at football practice and I found myself in a line to receive my helmet and shoulder pads. When I came home, my mother told me that I was to play football and finish the year. If I didn't like it, then fine, but whatever happened, I couldn't quit.

The season turned out to be a success as I fell in love with playing football. When basketball season came around, she asked me if I wanted to play and I said, "No, I am a football player." The next day, I had on a tee shirt and shorts learning how to shoot a basketball. I instantly was the best player on my basketball team because I used the aggression and will to succeed that I had learned on the football field. You probably can guess what happened when baseball season came around.

These lessons that I learned at the age of 8 were the key to my success in high school and college. My mother laid the foundation and supported me my whole career. She was the first to instill in me the character traits that allowed me to honor my family and my teammates. Being that I was the captain on almost every team I played, her lessons prepared me for leadership. I grew up thinking that losing was quitting and that was not an option for any team that I was a part of. I look at my team as my family and to this day, I use the same philosophy as a coach.

School was third because without good grades they won't allow you to play sports. I always took pride in my schoolwork because I knew how disappointing it would be to sit out because of lack of focus in the classroom. I knew of a couple of people who still were allowed to be around the team, and you can tell that watching was just eating them up. Most of them ended up getting serious about their academics in order to get back on the floor.

Having good grades also says a lot about a person's discipline and character. It says that you are willing to do what it takes to go beyond being just average. Even if you are not the sharpest pencil in the box, if you work hard, it will be rewarded. One thing I found out is that teachers are people just like you. If you come to them after school and go that extra mile, very few will fail you. I stayed on the honor roll most of my school days because if I was having problems with a subject, I would make sure the teacher knew I wouldn't settle for an average grade.

Even though basketball was a significant part of my life, it was forth on the list. When basketball becomes first on your list, you are setting yourself up for disaster. If you put it before God, you are neglecting the One who gave you the ability to play, and as I just proved, it can be taken away at any moment. If you put it before your family, you dismiss the responsibilities and duty you have to help your own. Place basketball before school and you soon will get a notice saying you are ineligible for competition.

However you choose to balance and prioritize your life off the floor, make sure that basketball is not number one. If you don't know where to start, then ask for help.

There always are mentors and ex-basketball players willing to share their knowledge and experience. I encourage you to take time to write down your priorities.

Basketball/Life Balance My Priorities

1. _____

2. _____

3. _____

4. _____

5. _____

Coach Godwin Tips

- **Focus on balancing your life.**

- **Prioritize you life. Don't let your off-the-court problems affect your play on the court.**

- # Always Keep God First!!!

Lesson Fifteen

Using Basketball to Score in Life

If you take yourself too seriously, you will miss out on some of the lessons to be learned from playing basketball. Basketball is similar to life in that it changes and evolves at each level. As a coach, there is no greater joy than for me to witness a player become a man through basketball. The lessons that you will learn in basketball will take you way beyond the basketball court.

Discipline: I am sure that everyone knows at least one person who has problems following through with the goals he or she has set for themselves. The root of the problem usually is a lack of discipline.

I remember being a freshman at the University of Buffalo and saying to myself: "Why do we have to wake up at 5 a.m. every morning to do conditioning? Why not wait at least until the sun comes up?" Well, the answer is that basketball was teaching me discipline. In life, you are going to come across obstacles and temptations. This is when discipline comes into play. Sometimes, you have to be able to "man up" and do some things you really don't want to do.

Communication: During the course of your playing basketball, you are going to have to talk to your teammates. Basketball is a game of constant communication. This is valuable, because in school the majority of your classes require you to be quiet and do your own work. The real world is the exact opposite. It's "why didn't you tell me that earlier?" or "Larry is sick so you have to finish his work also."

Another great thing about basketball is that it teaches you to communicate with people of different backgrounds. Every one of your teammates is different and you can't use a one-size-fits-all strategy. You find that you have to talk softly to some people and more bluntly to others. Communication on the court requires that you use body language and key words to get your message across.

One of the most important skills of communication is conflict resolution. If you play long enough, you are going to disagree with your teammates. In fact, it happens on a daily basis. Most problems on the basketball court result from a lack of communication. You think your teammate is going one way and then the next thing you know the ball is stolen. Your center is out of position and someone gets an easy basket. When you are working as a team, you all have to all be on the same page.

This is why I love watching Duke play. Coach K teaches his team to communicate and make adjustments. That's why no matter what roster he puts on the basketball court, you can rest assured they will be tough to beat. After every foul, you will see them immediately huddle up and communicate as a unit. They are a perennial powerhouse that is built on communication and trust.

Responsibility: One for all and all for one; this is the first thing I teach my kids when they come to play for me. If one guy is late, we all run. If one guy decides to mess around in school, we will run some more. What I am teaching my players is they have a responsibility beyond themselves. Every one of my players knows that every thing they do affects the team. Every player, no matter the playing time, understands that they all are accountable to the team.

Teamwork: You take a group of guys with different backgrounds and ask them to come together for one common goal. Our country was built on the philosophy of teamwork. The great thing about basketball is that you get to refine your ability to work as a team every day. Whether you win or lose, every game is an opportunity to get better as a team. I love watching basketball from November to March because each team matures in its own way. It is because the game of basketball forces you to work as a team.

Hard Work: How hard you work is the one thing you control in the game of basketball. As a coach, I design my practice to show me right away which players are ready to go the extra mile. I challenge them mentally with different tasks and goals. If they complete their goal, we move on to the next; if they miss their goal, then it's time to run wind sprints and start all over.

Hard work is more than just running up and down the floor. It is putting in the extra effort when you are tired and the odds are stacked against you. You learn a lot about yourself when things are not going your way. It's easy to work hard when you are up by 20, but what happens when you are down by 30 and fatigued? This is when you find out if you are a hard worker.

Will to Succeed: This is a lesson that every basketball player will have the opportunity to learn. Once you embrace the will to succeed, your life will never be the same. I call it the number one attitude.

I remember talking to a golfer at my high school who was the number two golfer on the team. As a freshman, this was a lofty feat but I told him it was not enough to settle for second. Every day I saw him, I teased him about being number two. It would be two o'clock in the afternoon and I would ask him what time it was. I knew he had two sisters, so I would ask him how many sisters he had. Anything to do with the number two, I teased him on. I didn't know it at the time, but I was stirring the will to succeed inside of him. His junior year, he ended up being the number one golfer on the best golf team in the history of the state. Now he comes back and teases me, but this time, every answer ends up being number one.

Strategy: Basketball is a very strategic game because of the constantly changing variables. Before the game, you have to prepare as an individual and a team. You have to look at whom you are playing against and strategize according to their strengths and weaknesses. This lesson will help you in life, because you naturally will prepare for the questions: "Where do I fit in and how do I succeed?"

During the game, you find that you have to make decisions on the flow of the game. Time, score, and position dictate your next move and what you should do going forward. Life is the same; to become successful, you have to be able to adjust on the fly. Just like when you miss a shot, you can't dwell on your misfortune; you have to concentrate on making the next one.

After the game, your strategy changes as you reflect on your team and personal performance. Every team and player makes mistakes during the course of the game. In life, they say that those who don't learn from the past are destined to repeat it. You learn this lesson firsthand in the game of basketball.

Dealing with Adversity: During the course of your career, you are going to run into plenty of obstacles. Since basketball is a team sport, you are forced to deal with all the issues that affect the team. Whether it is fighting back from a 20-point deficit or dealing with losing your best teammate to injury, you have to learn to take life as it comes. The thing about basketball is that you never know what is going to happen next. You can have the best team in league, but if your team doesn't learn how to deal with adversity, you are one problem away from disaster.

You also learn how to turn a negative into a positive. Whenever there is an issue within the framework of the team, someone has to step up. Every year, players are lost to graduation, injuries, and suspensions. In each one of these situations, the team has to adjust and fill the void. Pick up any pre-season publication and it is going to illuminate what each team is losing and speculate on its shortcomings. It is up to that team to find its identity and bounce back. They usually do.

The best teams use any form of adversity to become stronger as a unit. Teams that embrace adversity and use it as a stepping-stone usually achieve great things. One of the things I like to do as a coach is put players in situations that are not fair and just. Sometimes, it's not calling a foul and other times it's making them play seven-on-five. I let them know that everything isn't always going to work in their favor. If they can get through adversity in basketball, then life will become much easier for them.

Friendship: There is something to say about going through tough times with an associate. You will find that a lot of the people you compete with will become lifelong friends. When you are on a team, you form a special bond with your teammates. In pursuit of similar goals, you are forced to help each other out and look out for each other's best interest. This is where trust comes into play.

In college, as I was the captain of the team, I had the pleasure of welcoming the new guys to our family.

Since I knew very little about these new guys, I figured the best way to find out is to play pickup. With pickup basketball, there is no coach or referee to control how things are done. It was always the rules I set forth and I expected everyone to follow them.

One of my unwritten rules was to rarely call a foul. If I fouled you, I would continue playing just to see your reaction. Of course, this told me right away the kind of guy you were. If you complained and let it affect your game, then I saw that as a weakness. On the other hand, if you kept playing and didn't let me get into your head, then I knew you were going to help us win. It is these types of people that I became friends with off the floor, and to this day we have a mutual respect because we did battle together in the trenches.

Lesson Sixteen

Never Stop Shooting

Success is a journey, not a destination. Do not let the completion of any one goal define you as a success or failure. Like every young basketball player, my dream was to someday play in the NBA. Day and night I would work on my game, hoping to one day hear my name called in the draft.

I always will remember the day my coach called me into the office to tell me I was invited by the Orlando

Magic to be evaluated in a pre-draft workout. Right away, I was overtaken with joy because I knew only the top players in college basketball get the opportunity to work out for an NBA team. Most players have to jump through hoops to get into an NBA camp where scouts would come to see if there are any prospects they may have undervalued, but here I was given the opportunity to compete for a team exclusively.

My experience became bittersweet when I realized that my playing days were behind me. That ankle injury I sustained my senior year in high school plagued me my whole college career. I overcompensated for one ankle and ended up twisting the other. By the time I was a senior, I was playing on heart and basketball IQ.

Lesson Sixteen: Never Stop Shooting

My coach informed me that my medical history would be requested, and once anyone saw the chronic ankle injuries and therapy sessions, it would be an automatic red flag. I knew that this was the end, but I'm thankful to God that he allowed it to end on an NBA floor.

Excited as ever, I jumped into my coach's car and we traveled from Jacksonville to Orlando. When we got to the sports complex where the workouts were being held, I was led to the locker room. Feeling like a kid in a candy store, I went to each locker, stopping at the one of the man who inspired me to wear number 33, Grant Hill. I said to myself, "This is what I have been dreaming of my whole life."

The assistant came in to hand me my official NBA gear: practice jersey, shorts, and socks. I put on the uniform and immediately felt ready for the world. "If my mom could see me now," I thought to myself.

The NBA at that time was allowed to hold private evaluation sessions limited to four people. There were two guards and two forwards. One kid in particular caught my attention because he was just out of high school. I didn't remember his name, but after the pick-and-roll drill, I had to ask again. As I rolled off of his screen, I gave this 18-year-old a bounce pass, and while the ball was coming to him, he pivoted, launching himself toward the basket for a 360 dunk. After that play, I vowed to never forget this kid's name again, Amare Stoudemire.

Overall I had a great workout. The intensity level was high and I held my own. The NBA coaches get straight to the point and they test everything from your bench press to your jump shot. Those years of off-season training paid off and I was able to finish every drill. I left everything I had out there on the floor and to this day have no regrets. I thanked the Magic staff for the opportunity of a lifetime and headed back to Jacksonville to start JumpStartHoops.com, the ultimate source of basketball training.

When I look back on things, I realize that not making the NBA was the start of a new dream – the dream of empowering basketball players all around the world to excel in basketball and life. Sometimes when God closes one door, He opens another. Yes, everyone wants to play in the NBA and strives to do so, but you can't let it make or break you. I received a quality education (free of charge) and I now am using what I have learned to help inspire other basketball players. All said and done, basketball has been a great ride and a tremendous blessing in my life. I encourage you to keep God first and never ever stop shooting for the stars.

Lesson Seventeen

Always Follow Through

Now that you are beginning to increase your basketball intelligence, the journey does not end with this book. In order for you to become a complete basketball player, you must continue to seek knowledge and instruction. I strongly encourage you to log on to www. JumpStartHoops.com to join me in the goal of helping you reach your potential as a basketball player and student-athlete.

At JumpStartHoops.com you will find quality basketball instructional videos that will give you a visual of what you need to work on in the off-season. I recommend watching *The Fundamentals of Scoring* DVD, as it is essential to learning some of the basketball moves that were presented in this book. I walk you through the basketball moves and drills that you need to master to become the ultimate scoring threat.

My radio podcast, "The Coach Godwin Show", is a great way to increase your basketball IQ and hear more of the strategies that I used to excel on and off of the court. I go over topics such as: How to control your emotions on the basketball court; Developing basketball confidence; Be quick but not in a rush theory; Playing out of position; and many more great aspects of the game.

These are just some of the additional resources that we offer at JumpStartHoops.com. To stay updated on the latest basketball training information, make sure you submit your email address and subscribe to my newsletter. Until we meet again, work hard and study harder.

Subscribe Today to

THE COACH GODWIN

PODAST RADIO SHOW

"Basketball Insight and Instruction"

Your FREE Subscription at JumpStartHoops.com
will include Podcast such as:

How to Increase your game time shooting percentage

Conditioning and weight lifting tips

How to master the Mid-range game

The Pre-game mindset

About the FREE Bonuses and the

Basketball Training Podcast

Claim your free bonuses,
exclusive Premium Podcast content,
Basketball Training newsletter and
additional video tutorials today!
Simply log on to

www.JumpStartHoops.com

and submit your email.
No additional purchase is required.

Purchase

All-American Basketball
The Fundamentals of
Scoring

Learn the go-to moves that were presented in this book.

Learn the drills that will help to make you a better scorer.

Learn how to become an offensive threat anywhere on the floor.

DVD Available at

JumpStartHoops.com

Coach Koran Godwin is dedicated to developing basketball players. He founded JumpStartHoops.com to give players the insight and instruction needed to compete on a high level. As the All-Time Single Season Scoring leader at Abraham Clark High School (Roselle, NJ) and the All-Time Leading Scorer of the University of North Florida (2002), Coach Godwin brings a wealth of knowledge and experience to his teachings. He combines the rare qualities of someone who can guide with theory as well as practice.

Contact author: Korangodwin@JumpStart33.com

Photo by Brian Lusby   *Artwork by Kyle Ringeisen*

BUY A SHARE OF THE FUTURE IN YOUR COMMUNITY

These certificates make great holiday, graduation and birthday gifts that can be personalized with the recipient's name. The cost of one S.H.A.R.E. or one square foot is $54.17. The personalized certificate is suitable for framing and will state the number of shares purchased and the amount of each share, as well as the recipient's name. The home that you participate in "building" will last for many years and will continue to grow in value.

Here is a sample SHARE certificate:

YES, I WOULD LIKE TO HELP!

I support the work that Habitat for Humanity does and I want to be part of the excitement! As a donor, I will receive periodic updates on your construction activities but, more importantly, I know my gift will help a family in our community realize the dream of homeownership. **I would like to SHARE in your efforts against substandard housing in my community!** *(Please print below)*

PLEASE SEND ME _____ SHARES at $54.17 EACH = $ $_____

In Honor Of: _____

Occasion: (Circle One)   HOLIDAY   BIRTHDAY   ANNIVERSARY

       OTHER: _____

Address of Recipient: _____

Gift From: _____ *Donor Address:* _____

Donor Email: _____

I AM ENCLOSING A CHECK FOR $ $_____ PAYABLE TO HABITAT FOR HUMANITY OR PLEASE CHARGE MY VISA OR MASTERCARD *(CIRCLE ONE)*

Card Number _____ Expiration Date: _____

Name as it appears on Credit Card _____ Charge Amount $ _____

Signature _____

Billing Address _____

Telephone # Day _____ Eve _____

PLEASE NOTE: Your contribution is tax-deductible to the fullest extent allowed by law.

Habitat for Humanity • P.O. Box 1443 • Newport News, VA 23601 • 757-596-5553

www.HelpHabitatforHumanity.org